Mum's th

Meddy Ezrah Ortega

BookLeaf Publishing

Mum's the Word © 2023 Meddy Ezrah Ortega

All rights reserved.

No part of this publication may be reproduced, stored in a retrieval system, or transmitted, in any form or by any means, electronic, mechanical, photocopying, recording or otherwise, without the prior written permission of the presenters.

Meddy Ezrah Ortega asserts the moral right to be identified as author of this work.

Presentation by *BookLeaf Publishing*

Web: www.bookleafpub.com

E-mail: info@bookleafpub.com

ISBN: 9789357443050

First edition 2023

To my Kitombong and Kuwanyauma,

who calls me mummy relentlessly yet lovingly!

And to Kuya Alex who spurred the 9-year old me...

PREFACE

I've participated in the BookLeaf Publishing writing challenge to reinvigorate the writer in me. I started writing when I was 10 years old then life happened, and I simply stopped. I thought I was devoid of inspiration but I've come to realise now that writing like any other skill should be constantly practised to remain proficient in it. I am hopeful that this book of poems will be the first of many books I will write.

Mum's the word

Doubt clouds your mind
Fear grips at every turn
"Are you doing it right?," you ask
Unable to discern

She smiles at you
a gesture you return
"Am I enough?," you ask
Scared that the answer will burn

She takes your hand
Then suddenly you learn
Mum's the word she will always utter
Her love's the kind you need not earn

Quiet Revolutions

We wonder about the past
Overanalyse forks and turning points
Which exit should have we taken
To avoid the present that disappoints

We live, breath in the present
Stifle our tears, and who we are
How much do we have to compromise
To conceal and heal a scar

We look ahead to the future
Dumb down dreams, hold back desire
Will we ever willingly surrender
To the quiet revolutions that transpire

Windows

They say when life closes a door, it opens a window.
I boarded up the window to see if the door will reopen.
Then darkness fell…
For a while I was stuck in a box. Shrinking and deprived of air.
Wondering if the door was still there.
Praying that the window will be opened again.
Then light crept in…
 Slowly the box stretched into a room.
And then expanded into a house with two doors and four windows.
This time I'm shutting the doors.
I now know that unlike doors, windows, no matter what
will let the light beam through.

Happily Ever After

Real life is a fairy tale
A perpetual search for true love
A guiltless slaughter of villains
When push comes to shove

Real life is a fantasy
A constant wish to stay young
A pitiless judging of sinners
With gossip and a cursing tongue

Real life is an illusion
A daily dose of magic potions
A merciless expulsion of demons
Devoid of human emotions

Real life is make-believe
A persistent leap of faith
A ruthless elimination of lowlifes
Leaving no one unscathed

I Get to Smile Because of You

I get to smile because of you
I get butterflies in my tummy too
I get to wake up draped in sunshine
I get to sleep feeling fine

I get to smile because of you
I get to roll in laughter too
I get to wear fancy dresses
I get to enjoy life's excesses

I get to smile because of you
I get to skip with joy too
I get to travel and see the world
I get to go home safe & furled

I get to smile because of you
But I get hurt and cry too
I get to question myself and hide
I get to wonder why I'm by your side

Unresolved

I find myself wondering
Did I give you your due?
For all that you've done for me
Did I ever thank you?

For so many reasons
that could never be measured
For all the sacrifices
quietly treasured
For the love and care
that don't always show
And for the little things
that mean more than you know...

I may have not said anything
When everything went wrong
I love and need you still
I pray you've known all along

Subtitled

You keep your head down
They say speak louder please
You raise your voice
They feel unease

You say it's unfair
They say you don't belong
You demand to be heard
They sound the gong

You speak the same language
They still misunderstand
You utter the same word
Situation gets out of hand

You sit back
Accept the con
Enable mute
Subtitles on

Budding

I was born in the summer on the side of the
world where I came from.
But from where I stand I was born in spring.
That suits me better, I think.
I grew slowly and quietly like a bud.
Not held by my roots but by branches.
I bloomed unsure of my place.
Alone but among many others.
Blown by the wind in different directions…
Until I found a place to take root
Waiting patiently for spring to come again.
But deep down,
I long for the summer.

Poker

The cards are ill-shuffled
Until I get a good hand
I'm not taking chances
I've decided to win grand

You can spot my tell you say
that's a rookie mistake you've made
Now I know your weakness
And you're about to get played

Lifesaver

Swimming away will be quite exciting
Losing sight of the shore will be quite alarming
Being out my depth will be exhilarating

But

Not hearing you complain is daunting
Not helping you calm down is unsettling
Not having you hover over me is unnerving

And

Life will be dull without you laughing
Life will be bland without your cursing
Life will be bleak without you existing

Attempted Sonnet

Creeping into my thoughts and dreams
Is the way that you arrive
You're stuck in my head it seems
The more I reject the more you thrive

I invite you inconspicuously instead
And eventually find myself smiling
Suddenly I'm in over my head
But I cannot deny it's quite appealing

From the present I run and flee
Back to simpler times
When you're all that I could see
And love were simple rhymes

I need not look far as you're always around
Every corner I turn, our memories abound

Boundaries of a Badass

I wish I was uncompromising
How difficult could it be
To be tough, unyielding
Yet calm and conflict-free

I wish I could be decisive
How difficult could it be
When something's got to give
Let it go and agree

I wish I could be hard as nails
How difficult could it be
Stand strong when all else fails
Sturdy like an oak tree

Being badass should be boundless
But it's a fine line to being heartless

To the Books I Left on the Shelf

I picked you up because you were interesting
I flipped a few pages and I bet it felt exciting
When I sat down and held you
Comfortably with a warm brew

We could have gone places together
Faced all the changes in the weather
With teardrops smearing you
And laughter cackling through

I'm sorry you're gathering dust
Give you the time of day I really must
It wasn't my intention to leave
Thank you for the quick reprieve

Saboteur

Self-doubt is my strength
Accepting failure is my fate
Blaming myself my boost
Opposing happiness is my high
To fall into pieces my forte
Encouraging high expectations my habit
Underestimating worth is my wager
Regaling indecision my inclination

Living Epitaph

When people die
Regrets are high
Which makes you wonder
Do we really ponder?

It's time I think
to let it sink
that today's the day
for me to say

"We cannot really love anybody with whom we
never laugh, we sure did laugh."
Thank you for staying by my side.
For you, I quoted the most popular epitaph.

The Unromantic

I look at you and I feel secured
I give myself a pat in the back.
I've managed to erase my idealism
That in the past got me sidetracked

Who needs love letters, flowers, or chocolates
When you can have honest conversations
Why will you want sweet nothings
If someone accepts your imperfections

But the hopeless romantic is who I am
And it's struggling to survive
Now I've discovered you can be sweet
And it's only me that you deprive

Kuwanyauma

A beautiful butterfly who flaps her wings
Oblivious to what she brings
Like a puppet she pulls my strings
Doesn't matter how hard she clings
A flower blooms, a bird sings
She's the harbinger of all good things

Fire Exit

I've ran out of excuses to lay
This does not feel right anymore
Fight for true love they say
But there's nothing left to stand up for

They say, 'move on, you deserve to be happy!'
When I said I have, nobody believed me
I can't really blame them though
It was quite a feat to let you go

For how can one forget the past
When it made you who you are
When he made you believe that it will last
No matter how long, or how far

But true love does come by more than once
We shouldn't leave everything up to chance
It still boils down to choosing and committing
Give up on destiny or keep on believing

I still see you standing by the fire exit
But I have learned to shut you out
And now our memories fail me bit by bit
While my heart, for another, skips about...

Milton Keynes UK
Ingram Content Group UK Ltd.
UKHW020707231023
431165UK00016B/683

9 789357 443050